the GOOD LIFE
DISCUSSION GUIDE

the GOOD LIFE
DISCUSSION GUIDE

CHARLES COLSON

HAROLD FICKETT

Tyndale House Publishers, Inc. Carol Stream, Illinois

Visit Tyndale's exciting Web site at www.tyndale.com

TYNDALE and Tyndale's quill logo are registered trademarks of Tyndale House Publishers, Inc.

The Good Life Discussion Guide

Harold Fickett photo courtesy of *The Wichita Eagle.*

Designed by Jessie McGrath

Edited by Lynn Vanderzalm

ISBN-13: 978-1-4143-1138-8

ISBN-10: 1-4143-1138-9

Printed in the United States of America

12 11 10 09 08 07 06
7 6 5 4 3 2 1

Contents

Introduction

I INVITE YOU TO JOIN a conversation about the good life, about how the world really works, and about what we need to live well. All that is required is that you bring your mind, heart, and life experiences with you.

The Good Life and this discussion guide are for anyone who wants to discover the greater truths about life. We'll be exploring the deep questions that weave in and out of our lives: What makes life worth living? Where did I come from? Why am I here? What gives my life meaning? How we answer these questions will directly affect how we will live and how we will die and whether our lives will count for something.

Pascal once said there are only two kinds of people: seekers and nonseekers. This study is for seekers of any kind—young, old, artistic, poor, religious, or those who claim no faith at all.

Anyone who knows about me knows that I'm a Christian. I have strong convictions and can hardly claim to be a neutral observer. But I am a seeker too. My search led me into Christianity, and since then it has driven me to uncover more fully the truth that we are meant to know and live.

As I said in the introduction to *The Good Life*, I'm trying to direct the search without relying on any biblical assumptions. This may unsettle those of you who are Christians, but I think it makes sense simply to follow where human reason and the human imagination lead until we can follow them no longer. In the end we'll see whether reason and the imagination demand that their scope be enlarged through faith.

The Good Life is a memoir of my life as well as an apologetic. I share some of my successes, failures, and joys, hoping that my life experience may point you to the truth about life. But I also defend what I know to be true about the world and how it works. I believe a worldview must work practically to be legitimate, and I have found that a Christian worldview has the power to give hope and value to every member of the human race.

Recognizing that life stories are important, Harold Fickett and I decided to use stories as a major thread in *The Good Life.* There you will find stories from our own lives, from the lives of people we know, from movies and books, and from people who have shaped history. Thinking and living are bound together: We think in order to know how to live, and we learn what's true through living.

But your stories are just as important. As you meet with your discussion group, add your stories to the mix. Sometimes those stories will not be pretty; other times they will speak of growth and victory. In sharing and hearing each other's stories, we are challenged, inspired, and enriched.

As you share your stories, listen to each other. Respect each other's positions, and ask questions. Commit to being honest about your questions, perspectives, and beliefs. Remember to be humble. Above all, search for the truth.

To help you do that, we've designed this study guide with several elements:

- *This Is Your Life*—asks starter questions for discussion
- *Slice of Life*—shares excerpts of stories from *The Good Life*
- *Life in Paradox*—poses some of the paradoxes that govern the good life
- *Words of Life*—explores stories and passages from the Bible

- *Self-Portrait*—asks questions that help you move forward in your search for truth and articulate your own worldview

Study groups meet with all sorts of schedules: some weekly, others every other week or even monthly. We've tried to accommodate those needs by designing two six-week discussion guides. We hope that your group will be able to go through both discussion guides, all twelve lessons. If not, you can begin with the first six lessons and then decide if you want to continue.

My hope is that as you study *The Good Life,* examine your own life, and participate in your group, you will find some answers to the questions you are asking. I challenge you to test my assertions. Test your own as well. I believe that if you search for the truth, you will find the capital-*T* truth. And when you do, you will find the path that will lead you to the good life, to a life worth living.

Chuck Colson

DISCUSSION GUIDE ONE

LESSON ONE

FACING THE UNAVOIDABLE QUESTIONS

What makes life worth living? Why am I here? What's my purpose? Whether we are enjoying our daily routines or facing a crisis, we often think about these questions. *The Good Life* challenges us to engage our minds and explore our struggles so that we can find what really matters.

Are you happy with your life? Do you feel you have found meaning? Do you know what the good life is?

READ AND REVIEW
Chapters 1–3 in *The Good Life*

THIS IS YOUR LIFE

As a group, view the cemetery scene from the movie *Saving Private Ryan.* If that's not possible, read the scene on pages 6–7 of *The Good Life*.

1. Share some initial thoughts about what it means to live the good life.

2. What do you think the purpose of life really is? Discuss your responses.

3. Are any of us worthy of the sacrifices others have made on our behalf? Why do you think we feel the need to be worthy?

SLICE OF LIFE

Read aloud this excerpt from Chuck Colson's reflections on his first day in prison after the Watergate indictment:

> On July 8, 1974, my friend Graham Purcell drove me to a dingy Baltimore hotel, where four armed U.S. marshals picked me up and took me to prison. The meeting place had been arranged as a means of avoiding the press, but the media chased us from my home in McLean, Virginia, all the way to Baltimore. After giving my wife, Patty, a final kiss, I was put in the back of an unmarked car and taken to a prison on the army base in Fort Holabird. . . .
>
> Fort Holabird reminded me of a ghost town. The windows of its redbrick buildings and soot-covered, green

wooden shacks were boarded up. Rampant weeds clung to every wall. In the midst of the otherwise deserted base, a nine-foot chain-link fence topped by razor wire surrounded one of the wooden buildings. One thing about the barbed wire surprised me, however. It was tilted outward—as if it was more important to keep people out than to keep the inmates in. . . .

The prison building was a far cry from the regal surroundings of the White House. Paint was peeling from the grimy walls, and steam pipes ran down the long corridor through the center of the building, which was illuminated only by dim lightbulbs dangling every thirty feet. . . .

After I completed the processing, I was turned over to Joe, a swarthy inmate who spoke halting English. He showed me to my room, a nine-by-twelve cubicle tucked under the eaves on the second floor. . . . The temperature in the room was over a hundred degrees. Baltimore was in the grip of the worst heat wave of the year.

As I lay on my bed that night, trying not so much to sleep as to catch my breath in the oppressive heat, I wasn't afraid—at least not physically. I had been in the marines and had lived in just about every kind of circumstance. I'd always been resilient. I wasn't worried about the future or about making a living after prison. I was confident that I could get a good job in business or get my law license back, at least in some jurisdictions. The thought of having to live in these circumstances for the next three years was difficult, of course, but most painful was the separation from my family and my sense of helplessness.

But for me, the most shattering thing about prison was the thought that I would never again do anything significant with my life. I was always a patriot, which is why I volunteered for the marines. I had gone into politics motivated by idealism, believing I could make a difference for my country.

When the president asked me to serve him, I readily gave up a six-figure income (a lot of money in the 1960s) because I thought it was my duty to serve, to make this a better world. Now my own government had thrown me in prison. That cloud would follow me for the rest of my life. I would forever be an ex-convict. I had known the heights of power, helping to shape the policies of the most powerful nation on earth. In the future I wouldn't even be able to vote, let alone go back into politics, which I loved. I could never fulfill my dreams.

The story I had been living had come apart, and I couldn't find the ghost of a theme that might continue. My future seemed imprisoned—for life. True, I had thought of success in material terms—power, money, fame, security. But I had also seen success as doing things that affected how people lived. How could I ever achieve this now? I would always be a marked man, an ex-convict, a disgraced public official.[1]

1. Have you ever felt as if your story "came apart," as if you were "imprisoned" by circumstances? If you are comfortable, share that story with the group.

2. The most shattering thing about prison for Colson was the thought that he would never again do anything significant with his life. Have you ever been in a similar situation? Explain.

3. Colson mentions he gave up a large salary because of the call he felt to serve and make this world better. Why is it that we find

ourselves inherently drawn to such a call? What do you think this indicates about the soul of humanity?

LIFE IN PARADOX

Read aloud these paradoxes:

Out of suffering and defeat often comes victory.[2]

Prison turned out to be one of the best things that ever happened to me, which is why, on the *60 Minutes* program marking the twentieth anniversary of Watergate, I told a startled Mike Wallace, "I thank God for Watergate." Not only did prison radically transform my view of life, but the experience also gave me the one thing I thought I would never have again—an opportunity to serve others in significant ways. In my case that service has been a ministry to prisoners around the world.[3]

1. Reflect on your own failures and successes. Which experiences do you think have taught you more about life?

2. Colson also points out that suffering doesn't automatically erase our weaknesses. No particular virtue comes from just going through trials. In what ways have you found this to be true?

3. Share a story (from your own life or from the life of someone else) that illustrates how enduring great opposition or suffering can result in strength of character and blessing.

WORDS OF LIFE

The king seemed to have it all. He was on the high road of trade and culture, rubbing elbows with important world leaders. He was touted not only as the wealthiest man of his day but also as the wisest man alive. One would think that he had found the good life, but his inner struggles suggest otherwise. Even though these honest confessions were written centuries ago, King Solomon's thoughts speak for many people in the twenty-first century. **Read aloud** this story:

> I said to myself, "Come on, let's try pleasure. Let's look for the 'good things' in life." But I found that this, too, was meaningless. . . . After much thought, I decided to cheer myself with wine. And while still seeking wisdom, I clutched at foolishness. In this way, I tried to experience the only happiness most people find during their brief life in this world.

I also tried to find meaning by building huge homes for myself and by planting beautiful vineyards. I made gardens and parks, filling them with all kinds of fruit trees. I built reservoirs to collect the water to irrigate my many flourishing groves. I bought slaves, both men and women, and others were born into my household. I also owned large herds and flocks, more than any of the kings who had lived in Jerusalem before me. I collected great sums of silver and gold, the treasure of many kings and provinces. I hired wonderful singers, both men and women, and had many beautiful concubines. I had everything a man could desire!

So I became greater than all who had lived in Jerusalem before me, and my wisdom never failed me. Anything I wanted, I would take. I denied myself no pleasure. I even found great pleasure in hard work, a reward for all my labors. But as I looked at everything I had worked so hard to accomplish, it was all so meaningless—like chasing the wind. There was nothing really worthwhile anywhere. . . .

What do people really get for all their hard work? I have seen the burden God has placed on us all. Yet God has made everything beautiful for its own time. He has planted eternity in the human heart, but even so, people cannot see the whole scope of God's work from beginning to end.[4]

1. With what part of the king's pursuit can you identify?

2. Have you ever shared his disappointment that when you achieved something you had pursued, it felt disappointing or meaningless? Explain.

3. King Solomon asserts that he even found hard work to be meaningless and unsatisfying. How do you view your work? Does it feel like a drudgery or like a divine duty that has purpose?

4. What aspects of life do you find fulfilling and worthwhile?

SELF-PORTRAIT

1. Blaise Pascal said that everyone is either a seeker or a nonseeker. Which one are you? If you are a seeker, what are you seeking?

2. Do you feel as if you are living the good life? Why or why not? If you are comfortable, share your responses with the group.

3. After reading chapters 1–3 of *The Good Life*, what questions about your life goals have been raised in your mind?

Additional Notes/Questions

LESSON TWO

IN SEARCH OF THE GOOD LIFE THROUGH MATERIALISM

Shopping is not something we do just out of necessity anymore; it's a pastime for many. It often seems that the more we have, the more we want. As our bank accounts grow, so do our appetites to consume even more. We have an enormous drive to acquire and have all that we desire. We have more choices today than ever before, but are we really any happier?

READ AND REVIEW
Chapters 4–5 of *The Good Life*

THIS IS YOUR LIFE

1. Imagine you've just won a lottery jackpot of $20 million. How would you spend your winnings? Would you continue to work? Would you change careers?

2. How would that much wealth change your life? How would it affect your relationships?

SLICE OF LIFE

Read aloud this story about a wealthy man whose "good life" came apart:

> On October 28, 2003, a jury of the state supreme court in Manhattan watched a homemade video of the fortieth birthday party that L. Dennis Kozlowski threw for his second wife, Karen. The party, held on the island of Sardinia off the Italian coast, cost more than $2.1 million—or $28,000 per guest. Assistant District Attorney Ken Chalifoux introduced the video into evidence as part of one of the biggest corporate scandal cases ever. Kozlowski, the former CEO of the conglomerate Tyco International, and Mark Swartz, Tyco's former CFO, were accused of grand larceny and enterprise corruption for allegedly stealing some $600 million from Tyco.
>
> The birthday celebration included nearly a week's worth of activities, highlighted by the final poolside bash at the Cala di Volpe hotel. As the Kozlowskis and their guests gathered, young women in togas and bejeweled headdresses scattered rose petals at their feet. Male models dressed as soldiers and gladiators were also there to lend a hand—or a cheeky hug.

During the course of the evening, pop singer Jimmy Buffet performed at a cost of $250,000. While Buffet sang Van Morrison's hit "Brown Eyed Girl," Dennis Kozlowski danced his heart out. The culminating party included a laser light show in Karen's honor, a birthday cake with exploding breasts, and an ice-sculpture fountain, a replica of Michelangelo's *David*, that streamed Stolichnaya vodka.

A poolside ballet was the night's most lavish production. Water nymphs in gauzy dress appeared first. Then, to the accompaniment of drums, bodybuilders in winged centaur costumes rushed down upon the nymphs. They circled the pool, preening for the nymphs and audience alike. Then the male and female demigods joined in pas de deux, their dance celebrating youth, beauty, eroticism—their own divine powers.

The prosecutor introduced the video because he felt it represented one of the many excesses that Kozlowski allegedly engaged in while allegedly defrauding his own company and its stockholders. Kozlowski picked up half the tab for the party, but he charged the other half to Tyco, although no business had been conducted during the weeklong celebration. Kozlowski reasoned that since half the guests were Tyco employees, the company should bear half the party's costs. The government disagreed.

An alleged theft of $600 million dollars makes the Great Train Robbery look like a 7-Eleven stickup. The magnitude beggars the imagination, particularly when one considers that L. Dennis Kozlowski's authorized compensation over the ten years he served as Tyco's CEO added up to more than $500 million. How, according to the government, did Kozlowski and Swartz do it? And why?[1]

1. Imagine you were invited to Kozlowski's party. What do you think you would say to your family or friends during the car ride home?

2. What did Kozlowski's party reflect about his understanding of the good life?

3. Colson further explores Kozlowski's life, following his career to the top. After the tycoon moved into a $900,000 home and was appointed CEO, his first marriage fell apart. He quickly went from being a family man of North Hampton to wheeler-dealer of New York. How can the pursuit of materialism strain relationships?

LIFE IN PARADOX

Read aloud this paradox:

> My experience vividly illustrates that paradox lies at the very heart of life's mystery: What we strive for can often be what we least need. What we fear most can turn out to be our greatest blessing.[2]

In *The Good Life,* Colson shares candidly his rise and fall under the Nixon administration and how the Watergate scandal personally affected him.

1. Think about something that you strived to have only to find it was not what you needed. How did you deal with this truth and your unmet expectations?

2. In your own pursuit of the good life, what paradoxes have you found?

3. Share a story about a bad experience that proved to be a blessing in disguise.

WORDS OF LIFE

Sometimes our craving for more things is the result of our wanting what others have. We see their "good lives"—nice homes, new cars, money for vacations—and fantasize that if we had what they do, we'd be happy. One day a man asked Jesus to help him get part of his father's estate. In the exchange with this man, Jesus expresses some truths about what makes life good. In another scenario, Jesus warns against greed and misplaced trust. **Read aloud** these passages:

Someone called from the crowd, "Teacher, please tell my brother to divide our father's estate with me."

Jesus replied, "Friend, who made me a judge over you to decide such things as that?" Then he said, "Beware! Guard against every kind of greed. Life is not measured by how much you own."

Then he told them a story: "A rich man had a fertile farm that produced fine crops. He said to himself, 'What should I do? I don't have room for all my crops.' Then he said, 'I know! I'll tear down my barns and build bigger ones. Then I'll have room enough to store all my wheat and other goods. And I'll sit back and say to myself, "My friend, you have enough stored away for years to come. Now take it easy! Eat, drink, and be merry!"'

"But God said to him, 'You fool! You will die this very night. Then who will get everything you worked for?'

"Yes, a person is a fool to store up earthly wealth but not have a rich relationship with God."[3]

"Don't store up treasures here on earth, where moths eat them and rust destroys them, and where thieves break in and steal. Store your treasures in heaven, where moths and rust cannot destroy, and thieves do not break in and steal. Wherever your treasure is, there the desires of your heart will also be."[4]

1. Do you agree that real life is not measured by what we own? Share a story of a time when you didn't own much but felt content and happy.

2. Have you ever deeply wanted something a friend or family member had? How did it affect you and your relationship with that person? How did it affect your relationship with God?

3. How do you prepare for your future without hoarding your wealth?

4. What material possession do you treasure most? What gives this possession its value?

5. Jesus points out that our hearts focus on the things we treasure most. What are some of the things you treasure the most? Do they have more than temporal value?

6. What legacy do you want to leave your loved ones after you die?

7. What are you "stockpiling" in heaven?

SELF-PORTRAIT

We know that wealth and possessions are not negative in themselves, but they can distract us from the values and the truths that are even more important. As Colson illustrates with several stories, wealth and possessions, if they are used well, can benefit many people.

1. Are you happy about how you use the possessions and wealth you have? Explain.

2. If someone were to read your checkbook register or your credit card statement, what would that person learn about your values or the "desires of your heart"?

3. If you feel that your life needs to be rebalanced, what will you do to start that process?

4. What are you willing to put your trust in at this stage of your life?

Additional Notes/Questions

Lesson Three

Am I More Than What I Possess?

Finding the substance that really fortifies our lives is something that every human heart desires. Our culture tells us that money, power, and fame will make us happy. Yet as we look around at our friends and families who have bought into that myth, we find that many of them are not all that happy. What really gives us meaning and purpose?

Read and Review:
Chapters 6–8 of *The Good Life*

THIS IS YOUR LIFE

1. Who are the popular heroes of our day? What do they have in common? What special abilities do they have?

2. Who is one of your heroes? Why do you admire this person?

3. How does this person inspire you to live your life differently?

SLICE OF LIFE

Read aloud this excerpt from the story of Nien Cheng, who endured years of unjust suffering and torture in a prison camp in China:

> Nien and various interrogators would debate for years whether the People's Government had evidence that she was a spy. Her interrogators asked her to write copy after copy of her autobiography, hoping to catch her in discrepancies. They cited her friendships with British diplomats and others whom they suspected of espionage, but they could never prove their charges.
>
> Nien's position throughout her interrogations was based on one principle. "Am I not to expect justice from the People's Government?"
>
> "Justice! What is justice?" her interrogator said, scoffing. "It's a mere word. It's an abstract word with no universal meaning. To different classes of people, justice means different things. The capitalist class considers it perfectly just to exploit the workers, while the workers consider it decidedly unjust to be so exploited. In any case, who are you to demand

justice? When you sat in your well-heated house and there were other people shivering in the snow, did you think of justice?"

"You are confusing social justice with legal justice," Nien said, countering. "I can tell you that it was precisely because my late husband and I hoped that the People's Government would improve conditions in China that we remained here in 1949 rather than follow the Kuomintang to Taiwan."

"In any case," her interrogator said, "we are not concerned with the abstract concept of justice. The army, the police, and the court are instruments of repression used by one class against another. They have nothing to do with justice. The cell you now occupy was used to lock up members of the Communist Party during the days of the reactionary Kuomintang government. Now the Dictatorship of the Proletariat uses the same instruments of repression against its own enemies."

Yet Nien was convinced that a thorough and honest investigation of her case would allow justice to be done. She was so sure of this that she laid down the gauntlet to her opponents. One day she handed her interrogator the following statement: "I am a patriotic Chinese and a law-abiding citizen. I've never done anything against the People's Government. If the investigators of the People's Government should ever find anybody in the whole of China from whom I have tried to obtain information of a confidential nature, I'm prepared to accept the death penalty. At the end of the investigation of my case, when I am found to be completely innocent, the People's Government must give me full rehabilitation, including an apology to be published in the newspaper."[1]

1. Chapter 7 suggests that both Nien Cheng and Dennis Kozlowski experienced the consequences of a materialistic worldview. Explain.

2. Why do you think it frustrated Nien Cheng's captors that her life was not found in what she owned? How did she rise above materialism?

3. What truth kept Nien Cheng sane and hopeful?

4. What truths keep you sane and hopeful in the midst of difficult and sometimes unjust circumstances?

5. Chapter 7 says, "We often find true meaning and purpose in deprivation, when all the distractions of modern life are stripped way."[2] Share a story about when that was true for you or for someone you know.

LIFE IN PARADOX

Read aloud this paradox:

> Because she held fast to the truth, Nien Cheng, in her essential humanity, remained unaffected by the appalling changes in her circumstances. Nien showed her captors that it is possible to react in perfect freedom to a radically different environment. Once again, we see the great paradoxical truth: Our character is determined not by our circumstances but by our reaction to those circumstances.[3]

1. What character qualities were revealed in Nien Cheng during her prison experience?

2. Think of some stressful circumstances you are involved in at the moment. What character qualities do you see in yourself as a result of those circumstances?

3. What beliefs ground you as you face stressful stages in life? Share a story to illustrate your beliefs.

WORDS OF LIFE

One of the virtues of Nien Cheng's life is that even though she endured unspeakable injustice in prison, she never doubted that her life had purpose and meaning. Several centuries ago a young man faced similar injustices, this time at the hands of his own brothers. Jealous of the attention Joseph's father lavished on him, Joseph's brothers sold him out—literally. They sold him into slavery to some traders who took him to Egypt. During his time of enslavement, Joseph ended up in prison because of entrapment and was the victim of evil plots at the hands of unjust authorities. Yet, Joseph persevered, never allowing the injustices to affect his character and what he knew to be true about his life and purpose. In the end, he was promoted to a position of high authority and rescued his entire family from a deadly famine.

Read aloud the following excerpts from Joseph's story; in the first scene he reveals his identity to his brothers:

> Joseph could stand it no longer. . . . "Out, all of you!" So he was alone with his brothers when he told them who he was. Then he broke down and wept. He wept so loudly the Egyptians could hear him, and word of it quickly carried to Pharaoh's palace.
>
> "I am Joseph!" he said to his brothers. "Is my father still alive?" But his brothers were speechless! They were stunned to realize that Joseph was standing there in front of them. "Please, come closer," he said to them. So they came closer. And he said again, "I am Joseph, your brother, whom you sold into slavery in Egypt. But don't be upset, and don't be angry with yourselves for selling me to this place. It was God who sent me here ahead of you to preserve your lives. This famine that has ravaged the land for two years will last five more years, and there will be neither plowing nor harvesting.

God has sent me ahead of you to keep you and your families alive and to preserve many survivors. So it was God who sent me here, not you! And he is the one who made me an adviser to Pharaoh—the manager of his entire palace and the governor of all Egypt.

"Now hurry back to my father and tell him, 'This is what your son Joseph says: God has made me master over all the land of Egypt. So come down to me immediately! You can live in the region of Goshen, where you can be near me with all your children and grandchildren, your flocks and herds, and everything you own. I will take care of you there, for there are still five years of famine ahead of us. Otherwise you, your household, and all your animals will starve.'"

Then Joseph added, "Look! You can see for yourselves, and so can my brother Benjamin, that I really am Joseph! Go tell my father of my honored position here in Egypt. Describe for him everything you have seen, and then bring my father here quickly." Weeping with joy, he embraced Benjamin, and Benjamin did the same. Then Joseph kissed each of his brothers and wept over them, and after that they began talking freely with him. . . .

Joseph replied, "Don't be afraid of me. . . . You intended to harm me, but God intended it all for good. He brought me to this position so I could save the lives of many people.[4]

1. Joseph sincerely believed that God used his brothers' evil schemes for his good as well as the good of his family and an entire nation. Have you experienced a situation in which someone wanted to harm you but somehow good came out of it instead? Share the story with the group.

2. What was Joseph's view of the circumstances in his life? What was the larger purpose and meaning he saw in what happened to him?

SELF-PORTRAIT

Think about a time when you personally experienced an injustice. Reflect on the moral problems you faced and the set of circumstances you had to work out.

1. What truths helped you focus on what was truly important? What kept you going during that time? Share your story.

2. Do you feel the injustice was resolved? Does it matter?

3. How did you grow as a result of the situation? Do you see any purpose or meaning arising from the situation?

Additional Notes/Questions

Lesson Four

In Search of True Happiness

In our modern world, we are defined largely by our own choices. Our options are unlimited, and we are encouraged to exercise our right to choose what we think is best for us. We live in a time when we are freer than ever to pursue whatever we believe will bring about the happy ending. But does this hyperindividualism actually lead us toward the happiness we long for?

Read and Review
Chapters 9–11 of *The Good Life*

THIS IS YOUR LIFE

1. Think for a moment about some of the big decisions you've had to make in your life. What was the hardest choice you've ever made?

2. What choices cause you to be uneasy?

3. When you are faced with multiple options, how do you go about making the right choice?

4. What belief or worldview informs your choices?

SLICE OF LIFE

Before we can find the good life, we have to find what's good about life itself. John Ehrlichman thought he had an absolute right to define himself. **Read aloud** this excerpt from the John Ehrlichman story:

> In the summer of 1998, I received a frantic phone call from Patricia Talmadge, a friend of John's. "John Ehrlichman is seriously ill. He doesn't have many friends, and his family is not here," she said. "I'm trying to look out for him. Could you come see him?". . . It was then I learned that John's third wife had left him. . . .
>
> I traveled to Atlanta to visit John in his nursing home, noting how different this institutional setting was from his palatial home on the mountainside in New Mexico. Patricia met me and went to John's room to prepare him for my visit. He was suffering from renal failure caused by diabetes.

When I walked into John's room, I saw this once-powerful, imposing, distinguished man sitting in a wheelchair, wearing a cardigan, a blanket over his lap. He was only in his early seventies, but his health had been decimated. He had lost fifty or more pounds, and the skin of his face hung in limp folds. His beard was unkempt.

I felt a sudden rush of compassion for John. Nixon had betrayed him. He'd lost his power. He'd been disgraced and had gone to prison. The women who had loved him were no longer by his side. Even his kids were not around. This man who had once been sought out by the most powerful people in the world, whose wishes commanded hundreds around him, found himself desperately ill and virtually deserted. His world had contracted from his office above the president's to a lonely nursing home.

We had a long conversation. I asked about his children, avoiding the subject of his third wife. I told him about my own activities. As I did, I spoke of what motivates me and gives my life meaning, my faith.

He looked at me with the same pensive expression I'd seen so many times before. Then his eyes narrowed, and the light went out of them. All at once, he said, "The doctor says that with a little shot of morphine, he can put me out of things. There'll be no pain. I'll just go to sleep. Nobody cares about me anyway. Why should I stay alive? Tell me. Why should I stay alive?" His words came across slowly and listlessly, as if he were resigned to his fate.

Cold chills raced up and down my back. He was serious, and I wanted to give him the best answer I could muster. I struggled to choose my words carefully. A life was in the balance.

I told John that his life was not his own, that it was a gift from God. I assured him that his life was created in God's own image, which gave him an innate dignity, a dignity unaffected by circumstances. I reminded him that he owed it to his children to care for his own life. He would be setting a terrible example for them if he ended his life. I told him that he could know his creator intimately in the time that remained to him, that he could have a relationship with God and even experience joy, despite his suffering.

I don't know exactly what effect my words had, but he did not ask for an overdose of morphine. Patricia Talmadge told me later that my argument about the poor example he would be setting for his children had a real effect. . . .

John Ehrlichman died on Valentine's Day 1999. For the man who once held enormous power, there was no funeral. No one came to mourn. John had told Patricia that he wanted a "silent good-bye."[1]

1. In what ways does John Ehrlichman's story suggest that personal autonomy can actually turn against us? Do you think it is ever right to achieve happiness at the expense of others?

2. Reflect on some of the ironies of Ehrlichman's story. How did the way Chuck pursued connection with John show the benefits of denial of self?

3. Discuss the different worldviews illustrated by John's thoughts about ending his life and Chuck's response. Which worldview aligns with your own?

4. Do you think John's personal choices infringed on the rights of his children and family?

5. In your own pursuit of the good life, what does Ehrlichman's story teach you?

LIFE IN PARADOX

Read aloud this paradox:

> Walker Percy said . . . the self *cannot help itself.* This is the bad news, humanity's common denominator, and the defining element of modern tragedy. Those who try to save their own lives will lose them—that persistent paradox. Any worldview that cannot reckon with this tragedy can neither be real nor provide hope. Those who persist in believing that the self can indeed help itself must ultimately despair because they are buying illusions.[2]

1. Do you agree that the self cannot help itself? Explain your answer.

2. If self-perfection and self-focus are not pathways to the good life, then where can you look for help?

3. Tell a story about when you or someone you know found the good life by "losing" it.

4. Think for a moment about a time when you felt truly happy and fulfilled. What was the cause of your ability to taste the good life?

WORDS OF LIFE

Many centuries ago a young man was convinced that he had attained the good life. He was independently wealthy and held a political position that gave him power and fame. Yet he was not totally confident this was enough to gain him immortality. One day he approached Jesus to find out what more he could do to ensure eternal life. The young man was not very happy with what he heard. **Read aloud** the following story:

> A man came up to Jesus and asked, "Teacher, what good thing must I do to get eternal life?"
>
> "Why do you ask me about what is good?" Jesus replied. "There is only One who is good. If you want to enter life, obey the commandments."
>
> "Which ones?" the man inquired.
>
> Jesus replied, " 'Do not murder, do not commit adultery, do not steal, do not give false testimony, honor your father and mother,' and 'love your neighbor as yourself.' "
>
> "All these I have kept, the young man said. What do I still lack?"
>
> Jesus answered, "If you want to be perfect, go, sell your possessions and give to the poor, and you will have treasure in heaven. Then come, follow me."[3]

1. The man asked, "What good thing must I do?" Jesus made it clear that God alone is good and all good is derived from Him. What would our culture say to Jesus' claim?

2. What principles or beliefs do you use to determine what *good* means?

3. Do you find yourself identifying with this wealthy young man's inner struggle?

4. What do you think he was really yearning for?

SELF-PORTRAIT

Where do we look for satisfaction, for a sense of true happiness? Where do we look for the good life? The myth of personal autonomy—of "my point of view, right or wrong," of "my happiness, right or wrong"—is a mere counterfeit of what you and I really want. It substitutes an illusion of self-sufficiency for the sustaining reality of nurturing relationships within a community. The good life? We do not experience it in the loneliness of today's fads of self-expression and self-gratification. The good life is found only in loving relationships and community.[4]

1. Think about your current stage in life. Are you looking for the good life in self-expression and self-gratification or in loving relationships and community? Explain your value.

2. Which relationships and community involvement give you the greatest sense of meaning and satisfaction?

Additional Notes/Questions

Lesson Five

Living beyond Self

Finding the good life requires careful examination. We need to expose the lies of modern culture and ask if modern ideologies really work toward living a life of significance. Part of what makes us human is our innate desire to love others. We instinctively know that our hearts long for much more than self-gratification.

Read and Review
Chapters 12–14 of *The Good Life*

THIS IS YOUR LIFE

If you and your group have time, view the movie *About Schmidt*. If that's not possible, read the story in chapter 12 of *The Good Life*.

1. Why do you think it took Warren Schmidt so long to figure out what really counts in life? What triggered the change in his perspective? (Write your response on the next page.)

2. If you were going to your own retirement party, what would you hope others would say about you? What would be the highest compliment someone could pay you?

SLICE OF LIFE

Read aloud this excerpt from the inspiring story of Ernest Gordon, a prisoner of war who served on the infamous Railroad of Death during Word War II:

> The gruesome conditions were compounded by the prisoners' despair. Everyone was obsessed with self-preservation. The prisoners dedicated themselves to "The Ladder Club"—scrambling over others to stay alive. . . . Those who fell ill were thrown into a hospital hut called the Death House, where they were quickly forgotten. . . .
>
> Within six weeks of capture, Ernest Gordon . . . found himself wasting away in the Death House. . . . When the monsoon rains came, its floor became awash with mud. The latrines overflowed. . . .
>
> Gordon suffered from recurrent attacks of malaria, amoebic dysentery, the aftereffects of a surgery for appendicitis, and a case of diphtheria that had already paralyzed his legs, lacing them with ulcers. . . .
>
> Then, almost unaccountably, Gordon was among the first

recipients of sacrificial acts of kindness that eventually transformed the camp's entire culture. . . .

[His] miraculous recovery impressed everyone with the benefits of massage and simple physical therapy. Squads of men devoted themselves to massaging their ailing comrades' legs. . . .

Two engineers designed and built an artificial leg out of available materials. . . . Soon they developed a cottage industry that enabled formerly immobile prisoners to troop around the grounds.

Scientists among the group . . . began . . . gathering plants and fruits that had analgesic and anesthetizing properties. The homegrown medicines helped treat dysentery, vitamin-deficiency illnesses such as beriberi, and other ailments. The Death House began to function much more like a real hospital.

As a measure of physical health returned to more prisoners, their spirits began to revive as well. This expressed itself in a desire for learning. . . . They pooled the books and began both a lending library and a university without walls. . . . Eventually, men taught courses in history, philosophy, economics, mathematics, the natural sciences, and at least nine languages. . . .

As these renewing events gained momentum, the men became interested in whether a loving God might exist after all. A group of men who wanted to study the Bible approached Ernest Gordon. Did the Christian faith have any relevance to their current situation? . . .

Gordon hesitated because he had no faith to speak of. . . . Reading the accounts of Jesus' life in the Gospels, however, changed Gordon's mind and his life. He came to know a Jesus who had "no place to lay his head," who was often hungry, and was never favored by the privileged. Jesus had known in full measure the hardness of sheer labor, rejection, disappointment, and premeditated persecution. This Jesus had experienced nearly everything that the POWs knew as their daily lot.

"We understood," Gordon writes, "that the love expressed so supremely in Jesus was God's love—the same love that we were experiencing for ourselves—the love that is passionate kindness, other-centered rather than self-centered, greater than all the laws of men. . . . The Crucifixion was seen as being completely relevant to our situation. A God who remained indifferent to the suffering of His creatures was not a God whom we could accept. The Crucifixion, however, told us that God was in our midst, suffering with us."

The ultimate sacrifices of a few prisoners . . . transformed Chungkai prison camp into a vital community. With the least means imaginable, the prisoners drew together to produce the identifying marks of civilization: care for the sick, scientific research, broad education, and the arts. In the end they saw everything that they did and accomplished as originating in faith and returning to faith.[1]

1. What parts of the transformation of the prison camp most impressed you?

2. Have you ever been the recipient of sacrificial giving? How did such a gift affect your life at the time?

3. Have you ever seen a community or culture transformed by sacrificial giving? Share a story.

LIFE IN PARADOX

Read aloud this paradox:

In giving we often receive more than we give.[2]

1. Tell a story about how you have experienced the truth of this paradox.

2. For the sake of what ideas or relationships are you willing to give sacrificially?

3. Think of someone who is generous with time, energy, and other resources. Would you say this person feels a greater sense of purpose than others you know?

WORDS OF LIFE

Have you ever been surprised by someone's generosity? Maybe such thoughtfulness was from someone you never expected would even care about you. The goodness we encounter from strangers can be the very thing we need to point us toward what really matters. **Read aloud** the following story of a man who received compassion and tender care from a most unexpected source—a person from an enemy nation:

> An expert in the law stood up to test Jesus. "Teacher," he asked, "what must I do to inherit eternal life?"
>
> "What is written in the Law?" he replied. "How do you read it?"
>
> He answered, " 'Love the Lord your God with all your heart and with all your soul and with all your strength and with all your mind'; and, 'Love your neighbor as yourself.' "
>
> "You have answered correctly," Jesus replied. "Do this and you will live."
>
> But he wanted to justify himself, so he asked Jesus, "And who is my neighbor?"
>
> In reply Jesus said: "A man was going down from Jerusalem to Jericho, when he fell into the hands of robbers. They stripped him of his clothes, beat him and went away, leaving him half dead. A priest happened to be going down the same road, and when he saw the man, he passed by on the other side. So too, a Levite, when he came to the place and saw him, passed by on the other side.
>
> "But a Samaritan, as he traveled, came where the man was; and when he saw him, he took pity on him. He went to him and bandaged his wounds, pouring on oil and wine. Then he put the man on his own donkey, took him to an inn and took care of him. The next day he took out two silver coins and

gave them to the innkeeper. 'Look after him,' he said, 'and when I return, I will reimburse you for any extra expense you may have.'

"Which of these three do you think was a neighbor to the man who fell into the hands of robbers?"

The expert in the law replied, "The one who had mercy on him."

Jesus told him, "Go and do likewise."[3]

1. Have you ever been rescued by a stranger who displayed the type of sacrificial kindness mentioned in this story? Share your story.

2. Samaritans and Jews were openly hostile to each other, yet in this story the Samaritan puts aside all prejudice and takes the time to care personally for one of his "enemies." When have you found yourself hesitating to help someone because of your prejudices and preconceptions ?

3. Put yourself into the biblical story. In your life, who is the "beaten man" who needs help? Who are you most like: the priest, the religious person, or the Samaritan?

4. The story doesn't tell us what happened to the man who was rescued. If you were to finish the story, what changes might you imagine took place in the man's life as the result of the Samaritan's loving care?

5. What lessons about relationships and community can we learn from this story?

SELF-PORTRAIT

1. Think for a moment about your relationships. Mentally take note of how you balance caring for yourself and caring for friends, family, and strangers. What acts of kindness and service would you like to do for others?

2. Share a story about a time when acts of kindness transformed others' lives.

Additional Notes/Questions

Lesson Six

Searching for the Truth about Life

In *The Good Life* we've learned that pursuing pleasure, power, and personal autonomy can leave us empty, that only when we give ourselves to something beyond ourselves can we find meaning. Yet is sacrificing ourselves enough? An important question is whether *what* we sacrifice for is the truth.

But can we know the truth? Many people in our culture would say we cannot. Postmodernists say that truth is whatever a person believes to be true: You have your truth; I have mine.

Read and Review
Chapters 14–18 of *The Good Life*

THIS IS YOUR LIFE

1. What are some knowable truths that everyone can agree are true? For example, is there one direction that is indeed north? Or is north a subjective direction? (Write your response on the next page.)

2. *The Good Life* defines truth this way: "Truth is an absolute. Truth is what conforms to reality. That is truth's simplest and most elegant definition." How is that definition helpful?

3. What truths are up for grabs today? In what life circumstances do you find these truths at odds with your own worldview?

SLICE OF LIFE

Read aloud the following excerpt from the story of Václav Havel's stand for truth and his explanation of how Communism spread because of a society's willingness to believe in big lies:

> In the late 1970s the Czech playwright Václav Havel wrote the essay "The Power of the Powerless" as part of a joint Polish and Czechoslovak effort that resulted in a famous declaration of human rights known as Charter 77. Havel's essay was distributed first via an underground network . . . as people yearned for the truth that could be garnered in the Soviet

bloc only from unofficial channels. For this essay and his other activities, Havel was imprisoned for four months in 1977 and again in 1979 until early 1983.

In "The Power of the Powerless" Havel opposes Communism with no grand counter-ideology. Rather, he uses a common example of how Communism perpetuated itself and how it might be defeated. Take a greengrocer, he writes, who is asked by government officials to post in his shop window a placard declaring "Workers of the world unite!" . . .

When asked to post the sign, the greengrocer had to decide: Would he comply? He no longer believed the ideology expressed in the slogan "Workers of the world unite!" He did not believe that human beings are the product of their economic environment and that a heaven on earth could be brought in through changing social conditions. After forty years of Soviet hegemony in Eastern Europe, society had indeed changed, but only for the worse. People found themselves compromised by continuing to support what they knew was a lie.

In the government's view, fear that the people might discover that the Communist ideology was a lie was precisely why it was so important that the greengrocer post the placard. The placard kept him bound to the lie, and he became complicit in Communism's oppression. By participating in the lie, the greengrocer denied his own human dignity and made himself the servant of a false and imprisoning ideology. . . .

In his essay, Havel shows that the big lie of Communism could be maintained only by the millions of small lies elicited from greengrocers. The Soviet Union and its satellites became a vast world of appearance devoid of reality. Everyone who helped the system run had to act *as if*—as if economics determined destiny, as if the government protected the interests of workers, as if the rule of law were maintained, as if human rights were respected, as if freedom of religion were practiced. An elaborate system of ritual gestures—including the posting of placards in shop windows—had sprung up to enable the state's enablers to pretend to themselves and to others that Communism made life worth living.

For most people, this demanded an extreme compartmentalization—a public face and a radically different private face. In public, they acted as if they believed the lie, while in private they knew the truth. Greengrocers posted Communist placards because if they did not, they might lose their place as the shop's manager, have their wages cut, see their children barred from higher education, or face imprisonment. So most people in the Soviet bloc chose to live within the big lie.[1]

1. What are some of the big lies that our culture writes on its "placards"?

2. In what ways are we like the greengrocers who perpetuate the lies?

3. Why is it hard for us to stand up for the truth?

4. For Havel, the good life was living with integrity—recognizing the truth and then living within that truth. In what ways are you trying to do that in your life?

5. Tell the story of someone who effectively lives within the truth.

LIFE IN PARADOX

Read aloud this paradox:

> Truth became whatever one person believes. So you have your truth, and I have mine. This is the essence of the postmodernist era. . . . But if all propositions are equally true, in the end none is true.[2]

1. Colson asserts that we can know the truth. Strident voices in our culture would disagree. What do you believe?

2. How does a disbelief in truth affect the search for the good life? What purpose is there in searching for truth if there is no truth to be found?

3. Do you believe we can know moral truth? On what basis? Explain.

WORDS OF LIFE

Three lowly bureaucrats refused to toe a dictator's line. They were willing to live within the truth, even if that meant their death. As a result of standing for truth, they endured the dictator's full fury. Are these men hopelessly idealistic? Or are they fearless warriors for the cause of truth?

> Nebuchadnezzar said to them, "Is it true, Shadrach, Meshach, and Abednego, that you refuse to serve my gods or to worship the gold statue I have set up? I will give you one more chance to bow down and worship the statue I have made when you hear the sound of the musical instruments. But if you refuse, you will be thrown immediately into the blazing furnace. And then what god will be able to rescue you from my power?"
>
> Shadrach, Meshach, and Abednego replied, "O Nebuchadnezzar, we do not need to defend ourselves before you. If

we are thrown into the blazing furnace, the God whom we serve is able to save us. He will rescue us from your power, Your Majesty. But even if he doesn't, we want to make it clear to you, Your Majesty, that we will never serve your gods or worship the gold statue you have set up."

Nebuchadnezzar was so furious with Shadrach, Meshach, and Abednego that his face became distorted with rage. He commanded that the furnace be heated seven times hotter than usual. Then he ordered some of the strongest men of his army to bind Shadrach, Meshach, and Abednego and throw them into the blazing furnace. . . .

"Look!" Nebuchadnezzar shouted. "I see four men, unbound, walking around in the fire unharmed! And the fourth looks like a god!"

Then Nebuchadnezzar came as close as he could to the door of the flaming furnace and shouted: "Shadrach, Meshach, and Abednego, servants of the Most High God, come out! Come here!"

So Shadrach, Meshach, and Abednego stepped out of the fire. Then the high officers, officials, governors, and advisers crowded around them and saw that the fire had not touched them. Not a hair on their heads was singed, and their clothing was not scorched. They didn't even smell of smoke!

Then Nebuchadnezzar said, "Praise to the God of Shadrach, Meshach, and Abednego! He sent his angel to rescue his servants who trusted in him. They defied the king's command and were willing to die rather than serve or worship any god except their own God."[3]

1. Why do you think rulers like Nebuchadnezzar and societies like the Soviet bloc promoted their falsehoods—their big lies—by coercion and force?

2. What big lies are promoted in our culture by the media? by universities? by corporations? by leaders?

3. Why do you think Shadrach, Meshach, and Abednego were willing to die for what they believed? Would you be willing to die for a belief? If so, in what situation would you be willing to sacrifice your life?

4. What truths are worth dying for?

SELF-PORTRAIT

1. Write down everything that initially comes to mind about what you believe to be true about life. Don't think too hard, just state a few ideas that you believe to be true. (You may want to refer to this list at the end of the study to see what you might change.) Share your list with your group. Hearing others' lists may help you add to your own. Complete this sentence with a list: I believe . . .

2. Read through your list again, and place a check mark next to the beliefs that you feel you live out. Does what you claim to believe match your actions? List here some beliefs that you feel you are not practicing. (Write your list on the following page.)

3. Now look at this from a different angle. Think about your actions. Some of them may suggest that you believe something different from what you say you believe. (For example, what would your checkbook register or credit card statement suggest about what is important to you? What do your free-time activities say about what you believe?) Complete this sentence with a list: My actions say I believe . . .

4. On a scale of 1–10, how well do you "live within the truth"?

Additional Notes/Questions

DISCUSSION GUIDE TWO

LESSON SEVEN

WHAT IS MY LIFE WORTH?

The question of truth is a matter of life or death. What is the truth about who we are and where we came from? Does it matter if we arose from organic life or if we are the creations of a loving Creator? What gives our lives value?

In this age of unlimited progress, not only has the quality of our lives reached an all-time high, but our expectations have risen as well. We look at what we as individuals and as humanity have been able to achieve in the past few decades, and it takes our breath away. We often feel that life doesn't get too much better than this.

In some ways that is true. But it's dangerous to measure who we are and the quality of our lives by what we achieve. Do our lives have worth beyond what we *do?* If so, what gives life value?

READ AND REVIEW
Chapter 19 of *The Good Life*

THIS IS YOUR LIFE

1. When you see a child with Down syndrome, how do you feel? Why? (Write your response on the next page.)

2. If you live beyond an age when you can be useful to others, when in fact you are a burden on your family or those around you, what do you expect your attitude will be?

SLICE OF LIFE

Read aloud this excerpt from the story of Colson's grandson, Max:

> My wife, Patty, and I had a disturbing reminder of why the truth matters when we visited our autistic grandson's special-needs school, Melmark, one afternoon. . . .
>
> Autism is not the same thing as Down syndrome or congenital birth defects that result in physical deformity. Most autistic kids are as normal looking as their peers. Some do have a vacant, distant stare; others walk with an awkward gait from motor damage. Several of the kids carried computerized speaking pads that allow them to answer questions. These

children have suffered so much neurological damage that they would be effectively mute if not for these devices. . . .

When [Max] saw us, he broke into a big smile and started skipping with arms wide, looking for a hug. . . . He then grabbed both Patty's hand and mine and started to pull us into the school, excited at the prospect of showing us where he studied and eager for us to meet his teachers.

I was more than impressed with his teachers, who labor with him patiently hour after hour, day after day. They are paid a modest wage and work long hours under intense conditions. Autistic kids are demanding. Max, who is so gregarious, wants constant attention. He needs to be touched and held and loved. Many autistic kids, even in their adolescent years, do not have control of their bowels and must have their diapers changed.

At the end of each school day, when the students are dismissed at three o'clock, the workday is far from over. The faculty members gather to discuss the behavior of each student, meticulously planning the next day's activities. The student-faculty ratio is high: four teachers staff Max's class of seven. The job requires great physical stamina. The kids can be aggressive at times and must be gently restrained. Gentleness in this situation often demands as much force as several people can muster. . . .

The mostly female faculty members were all remarkably cheerful. In fact, they radiated joy. *Where do they get people like this to work in these schools?* I wondered. A survey of teacher satisfaction revealed that helping the children was the teachers' primary motivation; altruism is alive and well in this profession.

I understood their joy. I also have felt it as I've learned to love through taking care of Max. My grandson has taught me a lot more than I have taught him; he's schooled me in being a grandfather. When my kids were growing up, I was gone most of the time—too busy trying to save the world. I didn't enjoy the fun of rolling around with kids in the grass, not nearly often enough. Now, when Max is visiting or we're visiting him, my life focuses solely on him. There's no leaving him in front of the television while I go to my desk. At night, I can't just read him a book, say a prayer, pat him on the head, and tell him to go to sleep. In order to help him get to sleep, I play repetitive games with him, sometimes for hours. When Max visits, my schedule is Max's schedule.

The Max schedule makes me examine my priorities. It makes me think about the time I devote to *doing*—a lot of it simply indulging in distraction—versus how much time I give to *being*.[1]

1. Why do you think Max's teachers are so dedicated to the children with special needs?

2. Where in your experience do you see the utilitarian worldview—the maximum happiness or pleasure for the greatest number of creatures—at work?

3. What do you find seductive about the logic of utilitarianism? At what points are you at odds with this worldview? Why? What is the foundation of your position?

4. In what areas has our culture bought into the big lie of utilitarianism? How can you stand for the truth in these areas?

5. Have you ever wrestled with situations such as facing the disturbing results of amniocentesis or deciding whether to "facilitate" the death of someone who has an incurable illness or deciding how much money to spend in order to save someone's life? What worldview beliefs helped shape your decisions? If you are comfortable, share that story with your group.

LIFE IN PARADOX

Read aloud this paradox:

> Paradoxically, Max has introduced joy into the lives of his teachers, his mother, his grandparents, and many others be-

cause of these costs, these sacrifices. How should one account for that? How should Max account for himself, and why should he have to? Max is more than happy to be alive, thank you very much. Max knows a joy and wonder that puts me to shame.[2]

1. Why has Max's life been the source of joy for others?

2. Think about a person whose "quality of life" is limited (for example, a child born with physical or mental defects, a person with Alzheimer's, an immigrant who cannot speak English, a prisoner on death row, an unborn child, a person with an incurable illness, a social outcast). Share a story about what one such person has taught you about the value of human life.

3. Colson concludes that "the good life is not about the sum total of what we contribute to the world. It's about loving. Utilitarianism knows nothing of love. Love is the beginning and the end of the good life, however."[3] How have you seen this to be true in your life experiences?

WORDS OF LIFE

Valuing the lives of others, especially those whom society does not value, often takes time and energy. **Read aloud** the following story of Jesus' encounter with a sick woman, a grieving father, and a dead child:

> On the other side of the lake the crowds welcomed Jesus, because they had been waiting for him. Then a man named Jairus, a leader of the local synagogue, came and fell at Jesus' feet, pleading with him to come home with him. His only daughter, who was twelve years old, was dying.
>
> As Jesus went with him, he was surrounded by the crowds. A woman in the crowd had suffered for twelve years with constant bleeding, and she could find no cure. Coming up behind Jesus, she touched the fringe of his robe. Immediately, the bleeding stopped.
>
> "Who touched me?" Jesus asked.
>
> Everyone denied it, and Peter said, "Master, this whole crowd is pressing up against you."
>
> But Jesus said, "Someone deliberately touched me, for I felt healing power go out from me." When the woman realized that she could not stay hidden, she began to tremble and fell to her knees before him. The whole crowd heard her explain why she had touched him and that she had been immediately healed. "Daughter," he said to her, "your faith has made you well. Go in peace."
>
> While he was still speaking to her, a messenger arrived from the home of Jairus, the leader of the synagogue. He told him, "Your daughter is dead. There's no use troubling the Teacher now."
>
> But when Jesus heard what had happened, he said to Jairus, "Don't be afraid. Just have faith, and she will be healed."

When they arrived at the house, Jesus wouldn't let anyone go in with him except Peter, John, James, and the little girl's father and mother. The house was filled with people weeping and wailing, but he said, "Stop the weeping! She isn't dead; she's only asleep."

But the crowd laughed at him because they all knew she had died. Then Jesus took her by the hand and said in a loud voice, "My child, get up!" And at that moment her life returned.[4]

1. In the midst of the jostling crowds, how did Jesus show keen awareness of the personal worth of individuals?

2. What might Jesus' attitude have been toward the hemorrhaging woman—whose bleeding made her unclean, an outcast in that culture—if he had been utilitarian and believed that the governing philosophy for a society ought to be creating maximum happiness or pleasure for the greatest number of people?

3. Later, a man from Jairus's house reported that Jesus need not bother coming because the little girl had died. How did Jesus' actions demonstrate his deep love for all of humanity, even the dead?

4. Have you ever experienced or witnessed that kind of love toward society's "unclean" or discarded people? Share a story.

SELF-PORTRAIT

1. As you reflect on the chapter and the group discussion, what are some areas where you can more intentionally live out your belief that all human life has value?

2. Colson reminds us, "If we are here as the result of a random, chance process, then Singer is right; his ethics are, as he says, but a logical extension of Darwinism. If, on the other hand, we are creatures made in the image of God, then life has an ultimate value that cannot be understood within the context of a cost-benefit analysis."[5] How is the matter of where we come from related to how we value life?

3. If a friend who is contemplating an abortion because she learned that the fetus is deformed asked you for advice, what would you say to her? How would you articulate your worldview?

ADDITIONAL NOTES/QUESTIONS

LESSON EIGHT

TRUTH, BEAUTY, AND THE NATURAL ORDER

Where did we come from? What is our origin? What is our purpose? These are some of the most crucial questions we can raise because other answers about life can be discovered only after we determine why we are here. Scientists and philosophers hotly debate these questions. Did the world and the human race begin by chance? Or does the world speak of other origins, of an Intelligent Designer behind all that we see? What is the truth?

READ AND REVIEW
Chapters 20, 23, and 24 of *The Good Life*

THIS IS YOUR LIFE

1. As Nien Cheng watched a spider masterfully create a delicate web in her desolate prison cell, she was inspired by the creature's web-building virtuosity and thanked God. She was moved by the self-evident revelation that nature could not have, through some random process, produced a complex system capable of

creating such remarkable beauty. When we see the harmony and intricacies of nature, they cry out to us "intelligence and design." Share a story of when nature has spoken to you of intelligence and design.

2. Most public schools and universities teach evolution, that our world and humans arose from random processes. If you were defending this position, what arguments would you use?

3. If you were defending Intelligent Design, what evidences and facts about nature would you use to support your case?

4. Which arguments are more logical? Which one lines up with reality?

SLICE OF LIFE

Something about beauty—whether in nature or the arts—lifts us out of ourselves and points to something transcendent. When we experience the beauty of nature—whether we are walking along the seashore or surveying mountain heights—what do the awe and wonder in our hearts tell us about the world we live in? Was our world—from the intricate processes of a single molecule to the dazzling heights of snow-covered mountains—created by chance? Or are there signs in this world pointing to something, or someone, who holds this delicate and lively cosmos together? **Read aloud** the following excerpt from a story Chuck tells about sailing with his sons:

> Our very wonderings about the source of all things, including beauty, increase the probability that there is indeed something greater—that is, God. Nothing else could account for that wonder. . . .
>
> I discovered this at a point in my life when I was distinctly irreligious, at best a Christian in name only. I was on a lake in New Hampshire where I had taken a fourteen-foot Day Sailer to teach my two sons to sail. On one of our ventures across the lake, Christian, who was then ten, grabbed the sheet and was so excited over actually being able to sail the boat that his eyes sparkled. I was in the stern holding the tiller. I saw in my son's expression the joy of a new discovery as he felt the wind's power in his hands. In that unguarded moment, I found myself saying, "Thank you, God, for giving me this son—for giving us this one wonderful moment." I went on to tell God that if I were to die tomorrow, I would feel my life had been fulfilled.
>
> When I realized what I had done, I was startled. I had no intention of trying to talk to God, whoever He was—if He did exist and was even knowable. I was certainly not intellec-

tually convinced that God existed. But I had to admit that I was simply overcome with gratitude for that unforgettably rich experience with my son Chris, and I needed to thank someone—God.

At one level, it seemed, I couldn't conceive of His not existing. But I shook this experience off. I reasoned that I had been under a lot of stress in my life. Strange things happen.

What moved me that day to talk to God was an overwhelming sense of gratitude for that incredibly joyous experience. Gratitude, I have discovered, is built into every one of us. . . . When you wake up in the morning, lift the window, feel the fresh spring breezes, and see the sun rising in the east, aren't you filled with gratitude? I am grateful every day that I'm alive, grateful that I have a wonderful family, grateful that I have a purpose in life. Can you imagine believing that you didn't? If there's nothing out there except a great vacuum, why should you feel grateful for anything? . . .

Gratitude without someone to be grateful to is a meaningless concept, and no one's going to make up God just so he can thank Him. If there is no Creator, why do we feel gratitude?

The gratitude . . . I felt that day on the lake, the gratitude all of us feel at so many times in our lives . . . presupposes that there is someone to be grateful to. . . . The universal experience of gratitude leads us to know—in a way that perhaps only the heart can know—that there is a source of our being—God. My experience with my son in New Hampshire was the perfect expression of this knowledge written on the heart.[1]

1. Share a story of when you've had a similar "wonderful moment" or when you've experienced heart-stopping beauty and thanked God, instinctively knowing that He was behind the experience.

2. In what other ways is the truth about God "written on our hearts"?

3. How do the natural order, beauty, and the arts serve as a window to view the truth around us? What art form deeply moves you? What truths about life are more clearly communicated to you when they are communicated artistically?

4. If your life depended on choosing the right answer to the question of the origin of your world and all of its expressions of life—leaves and photosynthesis, young babies and the organs of speech, the world's oxygen-rich atmosphere and the intricate cells in your lungs—which answer would you choose? Would you say this world is a product of random chance? Or would

you say this world has been created by an Intelligent Designer? Why?

LIFE IN PARADOX

Read aloud this paradox:

> Paradoxically, the spider's ephemeral web had a permanence that the Cultural Revolution never would. Its dazzling display of craftsmanship moved Nien Cheng to thank God for the spider and all creation. It gave her a "renewal of hope and confidence."[2]

1. How can the truth we find in nature free us from the lies of culture?

2. Think about a time you were alone in nature and were refreshed. Why do you think just being in nature inspires us and can even renew our hope?

3. What does the spider's proficiency say about the created order?

WORDS OF LIFE

David, a young man who spent most of his early years out in the fields, tending his father's sheep, was overcome by the wonder of nature around him. He wrote passionate poetry indicating that he heard an Intelligent Designer—God—"speak" to him through the spectacular beauty of nature. **Read aloud** the following poem:

> The heavens proclaim the glory of God.
>   The skies display his craftsmanship.
> Day after day they continue to speak;
>   night after night they make him known.
> They speak without a sound or word;
>   their voice is never heard.
> Yet their message has gone throughout the earth,
>   and their words to all the world.
>
> God has made a home in the heavens for the sun.
> It bursts forth like a radiant bridegroom after his wedding.
>   It rejoices like a great athlete eager to run the race.
> The sun rises at one end of the heavens
>   and follows its course to the other end.
>   Nothing can hide from its heat.[3]

1. Do you think creation reveals that God exists? Why or why not?

2. What is unique about nature, making it different from anything made by humans?

SELF-PORTRAIT

1. If you are confronted by a friend who disagrees with your position about God's existence, how would you make your case?

2. If you were asked to make a case that humans are not the result of random processes, what would be your argument?

Additional Notes/Questions

Lesson Nine

Morality and the Natural Order

Just as the natural order informs us about our ecosystem and how to live in it, the inherent moral order instructs us about what is morally right and wrong. In the same way that natural laws prompt farmers to plant seeds at the right season of the year, our consciences lead us toward the right choices for our lives.

Read and Review
Chapters 21–22 of *The Good Life*

THIS IS YOUR LIFE

1. Think for a moment about a time when you knew you had made a wrong moral choice. Had your conscience informed you beforehand that it was the wrong choice? What made you go against your conscience? (More space on next page.)

2. What consequences did you face when you realized you had made the wrong choice?

SLICE OF LIFE

This particular story may be a sensitive, difficult one to discuss as a group. You may know someone who is involved in the gay lifestyle, or you may have chosen that lifestyle yourself. Chuck Colson chose this story not to offend anyone but to tell how a person within the gay community discovered moral order. **Read aloud** the following excerpt from Randy Thomas's story about his struggle with homosexuality:

> Randy saw in these [heterosexual] couples a contentment he had never seen before—one that was in glaring contrast to the desperation that characterized the lives of gay couples. His gay friends were always fearful and pensive, and their whole identity was wrapped up in their homosexuality. Gay couples involved in long-term relationships were still on the hunt for the next high, whether that meant alcohol and drugs or affairs or finding ways to idealize their relationship. The restlessness and isolation and fits of boredom that were part of the gay lifestyle never went away. The sexual encounters that allayed these feelings for a time only increased them in the long run. Randy's gay friends were like people who were trying to slake a thirst by drinking salt water.

The married couples at the Bible study completed one another in a way gay couples did not. By observing the heterosexual couples, Randy started down a path that eventually led to a number of surprising revelations. He came to believe that for a man to be fully a man—or a woman fully a woman—he or she must experience the ways in which the other sex is different. This doesn't necessarily involve sexual relations; it can happen in normal friendships.

Randy came to see that homosexual men are attracted to other men because they do not feel masculine enough. They see other men—rather than women—as essentially different from themselves, as "the other"—which is an illusion, and a powerful one. They look to other men to complete what they lack in themselves. . . .

In heterosexual relationships the differences between the sexes draw out the distinctiveness of each sex. Heterosexual relationships also balance the distinctive traits of each with complementary characteristics. The complement of male and female initiates a husband and wife into the true drama of sex: the creation of another human being. Every child is meant to be the literal incarnation of a husband's and wife's love.

Randy heard one of his friends remark that the birth of his children taught him what sex is truly all about. The curve of his wife's hip, his muscled shoulders that drew his wife's hands, the pleasures they found in one another's touch—these were nothing but costuming and scenery and lighting, the spectacle that accompanied the drama. The plot that gave the drama its essential meaning was the conception and birth of a child. Having a child together revealed the true creative power of sex, its profound mystery. Randy's friends' children directed the couple away from their own selfish desires and virtually forced them to concentrate on selfless giving—the key, as we have seen, to living the good life and creating a viable culture.

Randy realized that same-sex relationships can never fully realize this outward direction of affection; homosexuality does not lead either partner to love someone whose gender brings with it essential differences, someone who is truly "other" than himself or herself. Homosexuality does not naturally direct couples' affection toward their children, since this is a biological impossibility. Homosexual couples' desire to adopt children is a testimony to the simple human need to be outwardly directed. They know that part of their humanity can be satisfied only by experiences that their sexual orientation naturally precludes.

In many ways, those who suffer from same-sex attraction find their sexuality leads to an obsession with self. For example, homosexual couples often celebrate how they look, emphasizing everything visual, from fashion to haircuts to body sculpting. Because the visual never leads to the profundities of procreation, however, the visual becomes an end in itself, which makes homosexuals more attentive to the self. As homosexuals grow older, many become desperate to regain their youth symbolically through affairs with young men. Others find they cannot cope with their own idealized self-images. The sexual go-round wears itself out, and they suffer from depression, loneliness, and despair.[1]

1. What factors led Randy Thomas out of his gay lifestyle?

2. How does his story illustrate that the natural order also reveals the moral order?

3. What observations about the natural order (for example, our physical bodies) show us that a female and a male were designed for sexual union? How does heterosexuality fit with reality?

4. How should we respond when our inclinations go against what we observe to be the natural and moral order?

5. What aspects of Randy's story do you think are universally true? What elements do you think are subjective? What is admirable about his story?

6. In what ways have you wanted to rebel against the moral order inherent in creation?

LIFE IN PARADOX

Read aloud this paradox:

> Ultimately, the compromises that pity wants to make won't work because pity does not search to the depths of the truth. . . . The good life cannot be found in living in opposition to the natural order, no matter how difficult its moral demands may be. In the end these demands are the only path to liberation.[2]

1. When have you compromised your moral beliefs in order to be liked or to be viewed as tolerant?

2. What moral demands do you find to be difficult yet at the same time fulfilling and rewarding?

WORDS OF LIFE

Even though we humans are capable at times of locking up our consciences, refusing to acknowledge the truth, deep down we know what is right and wrong. The inherent moral order speaks deep within us. Such was the case with a man named David. He had shut down his conscience, refusing to face his own immorality: a steamy affair and a cover-up murder. But when confronted with a story about another man's self-centered scheming, David's conscience clearly saw what was right and what was wrong. **Read aloud** the following story:

> The Lord was displeased with what David had done. So the Lord sent Nathan the prophet to tell David this story: "There were two men in a certain town. One was rich, and one was poor. The rich man owned a great many sheep and cattle. The poor man owned nothing but one little lamb he had bought. He raised that little lamb, and it grew up with his children. It ate from the man's own plate and drank from his cup. He cuddled it in his arms like a baby daughter.One day a guest arrived at the home of the rich man. But instead of killing an animal from his own flock or herd, he took the poor man's lamb and killed it and prepared it for his guest."
>
> David was furious. "As surely as the Lord lives," he vowed, "any man who would do such a thing deserves to die! He must repay four lambs to the poor man for the one he stole and for having no pity."
>
> Then Nathan said to David, "You are that man! The Lord, the God of Israel says: I anointed you king of Israel. . . . I gave you your master's house and his wives. . . . [Yet] you have murdered Uriah the Hittite with the sword of the Ammonites and stolen his wife. . . ."
>
> Then David confessed to Nathan, "I have sinned against the Lord."[3]

1. What awakened David's conscience?

2. What cultural and personal forces cause us to shut down our consciences?

3. The Bible says, "Even Gentiles, who do not have God's written law, show that they know his law when they instinctively obey it, even without having heard it. They demonstrate that God's law is written in their hearts, for their own conscience and thoughts either accuse them or tell them they are doing right."[4] What is your instinctual, gut reaction to tragedies? to 9/11? to the Holocaust? to people's taking advantage of innocent children? to rape? What underlies those reactions? What does that say about the inherent moral order?

SELF-PORTRAIT

1. One of the big lies our culture tells us is that our sense of right and wrong is merely a result of cultural conditioning, not something that is inherent in reality, in how the world works. If you were asked to make a case for an inherent moral order, what would be your argument?

2. Have you ever experienced a time when your conscience became dull to what is right and wrong? Is it still dull, or has it been freed? If your conscience has been seared, what can you do to reawaken it? If your conscience has been reawakened, what led to that freedom? Explain.

ADDITIONAL NOTES/QUESTIONS

Lesson Ten

Do Postmodern Propositions Really Work?

Postmodernism would have us believe that there is no such thing as *the* truth. Yet what happens in a society that claims truth doesn't matter or that each of us has a right to our "own truth"? When we abandon truth, we end up with chaos. The absence of truth leads to an unworkable situation.

If we are not careful, we can be seduced by postmodernism, not seeing its inherent contradictions.

Read and Review
Chapters 25–27 of *The Good Life*

THIS IS YOUR LIFE

The Good Life asserts that most of us live in the big lie of postmodernism without ever realizing that it undercuts our reasoning. Postmodernism is a self-refuting process.

1. Congresswoman Maxine Waters marches in an abortion-rights demonstration because "my mother didn't have the right to an abortion." She doesn't see the contradiction in her statement. Naturalists believe their position is scientifically proven, yet in their worldview, the brains by which they draw that conclusion were formed by random chance. So how can we rely on that? What other examples can you give of postmodernism as a self-refuting worldview?

2. How has the irrationality of postmodernism affected your life?

SLICE OF LIFE

What happens when a person rejects the truth, openly defying it? Madalyn Murray O'Hair passionately believed that God does not exist, and she made it her life's mission to eradicate His name from public life. But in shaking her fist at God, she became evil and destroyed herself. **Read aloud** the following excerpt from Chuck Colson's story of his encounter with Madalyn Murray O'Hair during an interview conducted by David Frost:

> Frost began the questioning with me, reciting some of my Watergate misdeeds. . . . I began explaining how my new faith had opened my eyes to the true nature of my actions. Frost countered, "But you're a convicted felon, Mr. Colson. Why should we be listening to you about these kinds of issues?" . . . Frost then asked me to give my testimony, to explain how Nixon's "hatchet man" had turned to God.
>
> I had only a few minutes to tell the involved story, but I started talking, looking straight at Frost. As I was speaking, Mrs. O'Hair leaned forward in her seat and turned her head to the right, glaring at me just over Frost's shoulder.
>
> That was disconcerting enough, but then she started making grotesque faces. . . . She turned down her bottom lip and bared her teeth. . . . She began gesturing aggressively with both hands and mouthing words I didn't want to guess at.
>
> I've spoken in a lot of noisy and hostile places, from baseball locker rooms to prisons on the verge of riot. I've been heckled at political rallies. I should have taken Mrs. O'Hair's bizarre behavior in stride. But I didn't. . . . At first I dismissed her behavior as just adolescent razzing, like yelling to throw off the other team's signals. I concluded that this woman was genuinely trying to destroy my ability to tell my story.
>
> During the discussion, Frost . . . gave her an opening with a reference to the Bible. "The Bible," she thundered, "is full of murder and hate, the killing of little children. It is a brutal, horrible book."
>
> That was the moment that I had been waiting for, and I quickly reached across Frost and thrust my Bible at her. "Mrs. O'Hair, if you're going to characterize the Bible, you'd better quote it. You're a Bible student. Read to us what you are talking about," I said.

She backed away from me as if I had a weapon in my hands.

I pressed her again.

David Frost chimed in, "That's fair enough, Mrs. O'Hair. Mr. Colson's right. If you're going to talk about the Bible, why don't you quote it?"

"No, no!" she said, as she backed away farther, refusing to take the Bible from my hands. "It's full of hate and murder!" She would not touch the book. . . .

The debate ran for a full twenty minutes, and when the cameras were turned off, I felt exhausted. [I] . . . noticed that Mrs. O'Hair had gone off to a stool in a corner and was sitting by herself. I walked over to her, leaned forward, and said, "Mrs. O'Hair, I want you to know that I, like millions of Christians, am praying for you, praying that you will find the truth."

She looked up angrily and snarled, "Well, I don't pray, but if I did, I'd pray that you will lose. You will lose, Mr. Colson. You will fail."

I responded as calmly as I could that I might fail, but the cause in which I believed could not.

Why the furious response? If Mrs. O'Hair believed there was no God, why fight so hard against people like me? If she thought I was pursuing superstition, why not leave me alone, or even laugh at me? . . .

I concluded that the only reason Mrs. O'Hair could not leave people to their faith was that she really *knew* the truth. As I said earlier, I suspect Mrs. O'Hair must have once embraced the truth before turning utterly against it. Perhaps, then, succumbing to sin, she became evil within herself and had to try to destroy the belief system she knew was true.

That was my best guess, at least, and later, when I learned how Madalyn Murray O'Hair died, I realized I had met a woman truly given to destruction. . . .

Madalyn Murray O'Hair's sad and sordid life becomes a contemporary parable of what happens when you know the truth and give yourself to a lie. You become evil yourself, neither able to live a good life nor die a good death.[1]

1. Why do you think O'Hair was so hostile toward a God she claimed she didn't believe in?

2. How did her denial of truth lead to her destruction?

3. Colson says, "Mrs. O'Hair may seem an extreme and uncommon example, but in fact, we are all more like her than we would care to think. We all are guilty of denying the truth and living in defiance of the good. . . . We all sin. We know the truth but live in denial of it. We pursue the good life but consistently choose the opposite."[2] Do you agree with this assessment? Why or why not?

4. If you are comfortable, tell a story of when you denied the truth and defied the good.

5. Embracing the truth about life can be painful and even messy. When have you been surprised to find freedom when you have chosen to confront the big lies of life?

LIFE IN PARADOX

Read aloud this paradox:

> We know what is true and right, but we can't or won't do it. This is one of the great paradoxes, and it's the most crucial for seekers to understand. It's the one that fools us because it's in our very nature to be blind to it. This paradox . . . is known in theological terms as *sin*. . . . Our fallen nature causes us to do wrong even when we know what is right, and it can distort our vision to the point that we can no longer see the truth.[3]

1. Do you agree with this assertion that humanity has a sinful nature? Explain.

2. If you aren't sure the human race has a fallen nature, how do you account for evil in the world?

3. When have you been blind to the truth? How did this affect the decisions you made?

WORDS OF LIFE

If you were president of a new society and had to come up with a list of laws to ensure the well-being of your citizens, what would your initial list look like? On what beliefs would you base your laws? Would you point to any absolutes? Thousands of years ago God proclaimed His list of laws designed so that people could live in an orderly society in which family and future generations could prosper together. **Read aloud** these excerpts from a few of God's laws to His people:

> You must not murder.
> You must not commit adultery.
> You must not steal.
> You must not testify falsely against your neighbor.[4]

1. As the "president," how do you think your proposed laws compare with the laws listed above?

2. Are your laws universal, or do they apply merely to a few people at a specific point in time? Do you believe God's laws have universal applicability? Explain your answers.

3. Postmodernism doesn't want to recognize natural order, moral laws, or overarching truth. Many postmodernists want life to be whatever they construct it to be. "Don't tell me what to think or believe. I'll create my own truth," they say. What would it be like to live in a society without basic absolutes? Would we all be "free," or would our freedom be in jeopardy?

4. Many people feel that God's laws are too restrictive. Look at the four laws above, and discuss whether they restrict us or enable us to live more fully.

SELF-PORTRAIT

1. In your experience, where do you encounter the effects of postmodernism?

2. Do you see yourself as a postmodernist, believing that reality is what you make it to be? If so, make a case for your position.

3. If you hold a biblical worldview and were asked to defend your position, how would you make your case?

ADDITIONAL NOTES/QUESTIONS

Lesson Eleven

Providence and Purpose

Most people would express confidence that some force is guiding their lives. Some watch for signs, read the stars, trust in fate or destiny, and even expect chance alone to guide them. We humans have an innate sense that our lives are governed by something beyond us. Christianity calls this Providence, the belief that God is shaping and guiding history. Providence tells us that a good God is in charge of this vast universe and is profoundly involved with every aspect of our lives.

Read and Review
Chapters 28–29 of *The Good Life*

THIS IS YOUR LIFE

Some of you may have grown up in a Christian faith tradition. Others of you may have been exposed to a broader range of belief systems or to none at all. Think for a moment about how such exposure to various belief systems has affected your life right now.

1. Is there a faith tradition that you feel answers the big questions of life? Explain.

2. How has your faith tradition helped you feel that you are not alone in the world, that you are guided by something greater than yourself? Share your thoughts with the group.

SLICE OF LIFE

We all want purpose in our lives. We want to know that our lives matter, that we make a difference to others. When NBC journalist David Bloom was embedded with the American troops in the second Iraq war, he knew the dangers were great. But that was what he did; it was how he served people. **Read aloud** the following excerpt from the story of David Bloom's experience months before he died. Reflect on his beliefs about life and death and how he drew his conclusions about his own pursuit of the good life:

> When the second war with Iraq started, David volunteered to cover it. It was a risky decision. He and his wife were more than aware of the dangers he would face as a journalist em-

bedded with the troops during the invasion of Iraq. This was his profession, though, the way he served people.

Some months before David left for Iraq, he got into the habit of calling Jim Lane [a Christian businessman] every morning. Together they studied Oswald Chambers's *My Utmost for His Highest,* a classic Christian devotional book. According to Jim, David repeatedly talked about his complete joy as a Christian. He was free and forgiven: free to be the man, the father, the husband, and the journalist God created him to be.

David and Jim stayed in close touch during the time Bloom was in Kuwait City, preparing to move into Iraq. In his last telephone conversation with Jim, David said in a matter-of-fact way that if he didn't make it back, he wanted a message given to his wife, Melanie, and his three daughters. He wanted them to know how much he loved them, more than life itself.

Listen to David's sentiments in his own words, through one of his last e-mails to Melanie.

> You can't begin to fathom—cannot begin to even glimpse the enormity—of the changes I have and am continuing to undergo. God takes you to the depths of your being—until you are at rock bottom—and then, if you turn to him with utter and blind faith, and resolve in your heart and mind to walk only with him and toward him, he picks you up by your bootstraps and leads you home. I hope and pray that all my guys get out of this in one piece. But I tell you, Mel, I am at peace. Deeply saddened by the glimpses of death and destruction I have seen, but at peace with my God and with you. I know only that my whole way of looking at life has turned upside down—here I am, supposedly at the peak of professional success, and I could frankly care

> less. Yes, I'm proud of the good job we've all been doing, but—in the scheme of things—it matters little compared to my relationship with you, and the girls, and Jesus. There is something far beyond my level of human understanding or comprehension going on here, some forging of metal through fire. . . .

Then came the tragic news. David Bloom, thirty-nine years old, had died of a pulmonary embolism, possibly caused by sitting too long in one of the tanks.

Bloom's funeral at St. Patrick's Cathedral in New York City was attended by the entire executive leadership of NBC, by the hundreds of reporters who knew him, by the mayor, public officials, and by executives from across New York. St. Patrick's was packed, and the crowd sat in stunned, tearful silence as Jim Lane gave the eulogy, telling the story of his relationship with David and of David's relationship with Jesus. Jim read David's e-mails and quoted from David's favorite songs and devotionals. He concluded his eulogy by quoting Jesus from the Gospel of John: "Now is your time of grief, but I will see you again and you will rejoice, and no one will take away your joy." People who attended the service that day were deeply affected. It was a time of high emotion and powerful witness. In his death David Bloom had a greater impact on people than he might have if he had lived another fifty years.[1]

1. How did David Bloom's worldview and faith bring meaning to his life?

2. From reading Bloom's e-mail message to his wife, what do you know about his character and his life?

3. How did David's death bring life to those who heard his story?

LIFE IN PARADOX

Read aloud this paradox:

> Providence is often something that we understand only in retrospect. I look back on my life and see clearly the evidence of its invisible hand guiding my life at critical points—even before I was a believer. I took so much of what happened in my life to be my own design—my time in the U.S. Marines, law school, government. But I now see it instead as preparation for something much greater.[2]

1. What events can you look back on and marvel at how life seemed to work itself out? Do you believe those events to be coincidences or acts of Providence?

2. In what ways do you sense that the shape of your life, your relationships, your job, has been designed by something greater than yourself for a reason? Share your thoughts with the group.

3. Think about a person who has meant a great deal to you. What has this person taught you about life? How would your life be different if you two had never met? Is your relationship a coincidence or an act of Providence?

4. What does Providence reveal about the character of God?

WORDS OF LIFE

A truly good life looks forward to a final mercy, a good death. When we face death—our own or a loved one's—we tend to see life with greater clarity and focus. We sense keenly whether our lives have mattered, whether we have made our days count. We sense this in David Bloom's story as he speaks of the peace he had about his future—whether it held life or death. **Read aloud** the following excerpt from the story of Stephen, who had a similar sense of peace. Stephen had been dragged into court after several people had spread false rumors about him. Confident of his beliefs, he resolutely shared his worldview with his accusers—even though he knew that doing so might cost his life. With remarkable confidence and courage, he addressed his enemies with no regrets:

> The Jewish leaders were infuriated by Stephen's accusation, and they shook their fists at him in rage. But Stephen, full of the Holy Spirit, gazed steadily into heaven and saw the glory of God, and he saw Jesus standing in the place of honor at God's right hand. And he told them, "Look, I see the heavens opened and the Son of Man standing in the place of honor at God's right hand!"
>
> Then they put their hands over their ears and began shouting. They rushed at him and dragged him out of the city and began to stone him. His accusers took off their coats and laid them at the feet of a young man named Saul.
>
> As they stoned him, Stephen prayed, "Lord Jesus, receive my spirit." He fell to his knees, shouting, "Lord, don't charge them with this sin!" And with that, he died. . . .
>
> A great wave of persecution began that day, sweeping over the church in Jerusalem; and all the believers except the apostles were scattered through the regions of Judea and Samaria. (Some devout men came and buried Stephen with great mourning.)[3]

1. How did Stephen's very last acts show his character and reveal his good life?

2. For what beliefs or relationships would you be willing to risk your life?

3. Before you die, what things would you like to accomplish?

4. As Richard Neuhaus lay dying, he wrote, "In the destiny of Christ is my destiny; and so it had been all along, and so it would be forever. . . . What is now imperfect will one day be perfected in resurrection. The maggots should enjoy me while they can; they will not have the last word. Mortal dust already stirs with its longing for that great reunion." Why can people like Father Neuhaus and David Bloom and Stephen look death in the face and not flinch? What allows them to welcome death?

SELF-PORTRAIT

1. If you knew you were going to die this week, would you look back and feel that you had lived a good life? Explain.

2. If you knew you were going to die this week, how would you spend it? With whom would you spend time? What would you say to them?

3. If you are not confident that you are living a good life, what needs to change?

ADDITIONAL NOTES/QUESTIONS

Lesson Twelve

The Good Life in View

Where are you in your search for the good life? Have you defined for yourself what the good life is? Chuck Colson suggests that only a life lived in service to others and to the truth can be a good life. He asserts that the truth can be known, revealed in an intelligently designed universe whose moral order is simply a complement to the natural, physical order. Our reason, our appreciation of beauty, and our emotions powerfully suggest the existence of God and His care for us.

Read and Review
Chapters 30–31 of *The Good Life*

THIS IS YOUR LIFE

1. As you reflect on your search so far, what has become clearer to you? What questions still remain? Share your thoughts with your group. (More space on next page.)

2. Colson says, "Everything we have discovered points to the Christian worldview as the only one that 'fits' the way the world works and that fills the needs of the human heart." What is your response to this assertion?

SLICE OF LIFE

Chuck Colson remembers the moment when his life took on the depth and meaning for which he had long been searching. He candidly shares the defining moment when his life would never be the same again, when life became in every sense of the word, truly good. **Read aloud** the following excerpt from a visit Chuck had with Tom Phillips, then president of Raytheon:

> I had met with Tom four months earlier [and] . . . had been impressed that day with how much he had changed from the man I had known before I went to the White House. Tom had seemed very much at peace with himself. I had asked him what happened to him. I can remember to this day his exact words: "Chuck, I have accepted Jesus Christ and committed my life to Him." I nervously changed the subject. I'd never before heard anyone talk that way. In my mind, Jesus

was merely an ancient historical figure. But in the months that followed, I couldn't get Tom's words out of my mind.

So . . . I met with Tom at his home. I wanted him to explain what had happened in his life. *Maybe, just maybe,* I thought, *he might help me.* . . .

He described to me what had happened to him. Some years earlier he had gone to a Billy Graham crusade in New York and found himself strangely moved by the message. He was so moved that at the end, when Graham gave an invitation to accept Christ as one's personal Lord and Savior, Tom Phillips walked forward with hundreds of others and surrendered his life to Christ. He then described how his life had been dramatically transformed.

As he told me his story, he pulled a paperback book off the table next to him and asked if he might read a chapter to me. The book was *Mere Christianity,* C. S. Lewis's classic work, and the chapter that Phillips read from was titled "The Great Sin." Pride.

Tom's reading of that chapter was for me a totally devastating moment. I saw myself and my life captured in Lewis's incredible words about that great sin that we quickly see in others but rarely recognize in ourselves: the haughty, arrogant attitude that comes from building our life around ourselves.

As Phillips was reading, . . . [my] life experiences were flashing across my mind, just like the movie scenes where people see their lives lived out in the instant before they die. I now realize that I was, in a sense, about to die.

I thought about my insufferable arrogance. Oh, sure, I had done good deeds for people and took care of the underdog. . . . I was a pretty decent guy, so I thought. In truth, my smug sense of self-righteousness hid my total self-obsession.

Through the years in which I rose quickly in law and politics at the cost of my first marriage, I justified everything.

I told myself I was doing it all for my family and my country, for national security. I was convinced that it was all a selfless endeavor. I realized that night at Tom's house that it had all been about me.

As Tom read Lewis's words, some of them hit me with particular force, shattering the defense mechanism I'd built up over all of those years—the tough-guy exterior. The truth suddenly made sense. As C. S. Lewis wrote, someone who is so proud and so wrapped up in himself and so capable of rationalizing anything could not possibly see something immeasurably greater than himself—God.

I was so uncomfortable that I couldn't wait to get out of Tom's home that night. He asked me if he could pray for me, and he did, a prayer like I'd never heard in church. Like I'd never heard anywhere. It was warm, moving, and caring. And what struck me as much as anything else was that Tom Phillips, one of the busiest, most successful businessmen in America, really, genuinely cared for me, Chuck Colson. Not the big-time Washington operator, but Chuck Colson the human being.

I said good-bye to Tom and headed for my car, but . . . I felt a sudden desperate desire to go back and pray again with Tom Phillips. I turned around and looked at the house, but the lights downstairs were already going out. Too late, I realized. So I got in the car, started the ignition, and drove out of the driveway. I could get no farther than a hundred yards from his house, however, because I was crying too hard to drive the car. The former marine captain, the tough White House "hatchet man" who thought he was as good as or better than anybody else, felt wretched.

For the first time in my life I had looked inside of my own heart and detested what I saw. It was corrupt. I thought of the people I had hurt, the wrong I had done to others, how cold, hard, and self-centered I was. For the very first time in my life, I was deeply convicted of my own sin. I felt unclean, ashamed, horribly alone and horribly lost. Tom's words kept flowing over me about turning to God and making that simple surrender. I found myself in those moments almost involuntarily crying out: "God, I don't know the right words, and I'm not much, but please take me. Take me just the way I am." I sat there for half an hour, perhaps an hour, alone with my thoughts, tears flowing freely as they had never done before in my life. I experienced a feeling of total surrender and total release. I knew at that moment God was real, personal, and had heard my prayers.[1]

1. How can pride keep us from finding the good life?

2. Colson finally finds the good life when he recognizes the depth of his own pride, surrenders himself to God, and cries out for help. Have you ever had that experience? If so, share your story with your group. If not, what keeps you from surrendering?

3. After reading the rational arguments and stories in this book, do you find yourself persuaded to further seek God and His truth? Why or why not?

4. Colson says that the gospel message is "maddeningly simple." Have you found this to be true for you? If not, what part of Christianity is difficult to accept or understand?

LIFE IN PARADOX

Read aloud this paradox:

> But we have to confront one last, stunning, paradoxical truth: You cannot find the good life through searching alone. You have to be found by God. In the end, all seekers discover that while they thought they were searching for God, God was searching for them. He longs for us and pursues us.
>
> That's why reason alone falls short. The sin that is in our nature corrupts our will, . . . [and only] God transforms the will. . . .
>
> The search prepares the heart to accept the true object of its longing—the God whose love the human heart desires.

The search also reveals our inner rebellion; it shows us our need to surrender to God's consuming embrace. We must offer ourselves to God through His gift to us—faith.[2]

1. Although reason is a powerful force in our search for the truth, it is not enough. In the end the search must include the leap of faith. God cannot reveal Himself to us in a rationally irrefutable matter. What role have faith and reason played in your search for truth?

2. What evidence do you have from your own experience that God is searching for you and that He pursues you?

3. How does the search for the good life prepare the heart to accept God's consuming embrace?

WORDS OF LIFE

Dissatisfied with life under his father's roof, a young man asks his father for his share of the inheritance so that he can pursue the good life. **Read aloud** the following story of what happens to the young man and his father:

> To illustrate the point further, Jesus told them this story: "A man had two sons. The younger son told his father, 'I want my share of your estate now before you die.' So his father agreed to divide his wealth between his sons.
>
> "A few days later this younger son packed all his belongings and moved to a distant land, and there he wasted all his money in wild living. About the time his money ran out, a great famine swept over the land, and he began to starve. He persuaded a local farmer to hire him, and the man sent him into his fields to feed the pigs. The young man became so hungry that even the pods he was feeding the pigs looked good to him. But no one gave him anything.
>
> "When he finally came to his senses, he said to himself, 'At home even the hired servants have food enough to spare, and here I am dying of hunger! I will go home to my father and say, "Father, I have sinned against both heaven and you, and I am no longer worthy of being called your son. Please take me on as a hired servant."'
>
> "So he returned home to his father. And while he was still a long way off, his father saw him coming. Filled with love and compassion, he ran to his son, embraced him, and kissed him. His son said to him, 'Father, I have sinned against both heaven and you, and I am no longer worthy of being called your son.'
>
> "But his father said to the servants, 'Quick! Bring the finest robe in the house and put it on him. Get a ring for his fin-

ger and sandals for his feet. And kill the calf we have been fattening. We must celebrate with a feast, for this son of mine was dead and has now returned to life. He was lost, but now he is found.' So the party began."[3]

1. What did the younger son learn about the good life?

2. In the cultural context of the day, the son's request for getting his inheritance early was tantamount to saying to his father, "I wish you were dead." What would you expect the father's response to be when his son returns from having squandered the inheritance?

3. How does the father's response reflect God's attitude toward us when we realize we have looked in the wrong places for the good life and want to come "home"?

SELF-PORTRAIT

1. If you have not already done so, share your life story with your group. For those who are Christians, explain how you found God to be the answer for your life. For those who are still seeking the good life, share your experience of pursuing truth.

2. Where are you in your search for truth? Have you found the capital-*T* truth? Maybe you are like Chuck Colson in the story at the beginning of this lesson, longing for the peace you see in the lives of others. Maybe you are looking for a person like Tom Phillips, a person who can talk with you and pray for you. Or maybe you are at the point where you want to cry out to God as Chuck did, "God, I don't know the right words, and I'm not much, but please take me. Take me just the way I am." You can pray to God and offer yourself to Him, just the way you are. Like the father in the story, God is waiting for you with open arms. He will embrace you with His love and compassion. If you want someone to pray with you, as Tom Phillips did for Chuck, ask someone in your group to share that moment with you.

3. If you have already given yourself to Christ, think about some next steps. Have you unknowingly bought into some of the cultural lies? Have you lost your sense of service to others? Have you missed opportunities to stand for the Truth? How can you take steps toward growth? Ask God to give you direction in how to live the truly good life.

ADDITIONAL NOTES/QUESTIONS

Notes

Lesson 1: Facing the Unavoidable Questions

1. Charles Colson with Harold Fickett, *The Good Life* (Wheaton, Ill.: Tyndale, 2005), 20–22.
2. *The Good Life*, 23.
3. Ibid.
4. Ecclesiastes 2:1-11; 3:9-11.

Lesson 2: In Search of the Good Life through Materialism

1. *The Good Life*, 35–36.
2. Ibid., 23.
3. Luke 12:13-21.
4. Matthew 6:19-21.

Lesson 3: Am I More Than What I Possess?

1. *The Good Life*, 64.
2. Ibid., 76.
3. Ibid., 74.
4. Genesis 45:1-15; 50:19-20. To read the entire story of Joseph, read Genesis 37–50.

Lesson 4: In Search of True Happiness

1. *The Good Life*, 98–100.
2. Ibid., 112.
3. Matthew 19:16-21, NIV.
4. *The Good Life*, 120.

Lesson 5: Living beyond Self

1. *The Good Life*, 147–153.
2. Ibid., 138.
3. Luke 10:25-37, NIV.

Lesson 6: Searching for the Truth about Life

1. *The Good Life*, 180–182.
2. Ibid., 187.
3. Daniel 3:14-20, 25-28.

LESSON 7: WHAT IS MY LIFE WORTH?
1. *The Good Life*, 197–199.
2. Ibid., 211.
3. Ibid.
4. Luke 8:40-55.
5. *The Good Life*, 212.

LESSON 8: TRUTH, BEAUTY, AND THE NATURAL ORDER
1. *The Good Life*, 271–273.
2. Ibid., 214.
3. Psalm 19:1-6.

LESSON 9: MORALITY AND THE NATURAL ORDER
1. *The Good Life*, 239–241.
2. Ibid., 244–245.
3. 2 Samuel 11:27–12:13.
4. Romans 2:14-15.

LESSON 10: DO POSTMODERN PROPOSITIONS REALLY WORK?
1. *The Good Life*, 308–310, 315.
2. Ibid., 315–316.
3. Ibid., 306.
4. Exodus 20:13-16.

LESSON 11: PROVIDENCE AND PURPOSE
1. *The Good Life*, 343–344.
2. Ibid., 322–323.
3. Acts 7:54–8:1-2.

LESSON 12: THE GOOD LIFE IN VIEW
1. *The Good Life*, 351–354.
2. Ibid., 348.
3. Luke 15:11-24.

About the Authors

Charles W. Colson is a popular and widely known author, speaker, and radio commentator. A former presidential aide to Richard Nixon and founder of the international Prison Fellowship Prison Ministries, he has written many books, including *Born Again, Loving God, Being the Body* (with Ellen Vaughn), and *How Now Shall We Live?* (coauthor, Nancy Pearcey).

In 1993 Colson was awarded the Templeton Prize for Progress in Religion, given for extraordinary leadership and originality in advancing humanity's understanding of God.

Harold Fickett is a full-time writer and the author of novels, biographies, and works of spirituality, including *The Holy Fool, The Living Christ, Dancing with the Divine,* and a forthcoming biography of Albert Schweitzer. Fickett has collaborated with Colson on several books, including the contemporary classics *Loving God* and *How Now Shall We Live?* He is also a contributing editor of *Godspy* (www.godspy.com), where he writes columns on world Christianity and spirituality.

Other Tyndale books by CHARLES COLSON

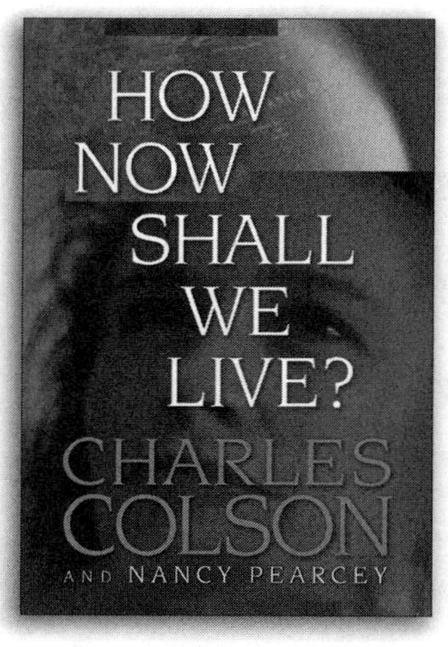

How Now Shall We Live? The classic best seller that has changed the way hundreds of thousands of people think about life, truth, and faith.

Lies That Go Unchallenged in Popular Culture
Provocative examinations of the messages that popular culture propagates and how they mislead millions of people.

SOFTCOVER

Lies That Go Unchallenged in Media & Government
A look at the dangerous worldviews that media and government preach and how these views undermine truth and faith.

SOFTCOVER

To discover more about *the good life*, read Charles Colson's new book

From his own life and through the extraordinary lives of others, Chuck Colson paints vivid portraits of people, examines what they live for, and evaluates what really provides purpose, meaning, and truth in life.

Visit Charles Colson's *The Good Life* Web site at **www.goodlifethebook.com** for tools to share *The Good Life* with others.